Poems –
Songs and Letters

Poems –
Songs and Letters

Volume III

Keith Vance

POEMS - SONGS AND LETTERS: VOLUME III

This book is written to provide information and motivation to readers. Its purpose is not to render any type of psychological, legal, or professional advice of any kind. The content is the sole opinion and expression of the author, and not necessarily that of the publisher.

Copyright © 2019 by Keith Vance

All rights reserved. No part of this book may be reproduced, transmitted, or distributed in any form by any means, including, but not limited to, recording, photocopying, or taking screenshots of parts of the book, without prior written permission from the author or the publisher. Brief quotations for noncommercial purposes, such as book reviews, permitted by Fair Use of the U.S. Copyright Law, are allowed without written permissions, as long as such quotations do not cause damage to the book's commercial value. For permissions, write to the publisher, whose address is stated below.

Printed in the United States of America.

ISBN   978-1-64552-140-2   (Paperback)
ISBN   978-1-64552-141-9   (Digital)

Lettra Press books may be ordered through booksellers or by contacting:

Lettra Press LLC
18601 Green Valley Ranch Blvd.
Unit 108, Box 204 Denver, CO 80249
1 303 586 1431 | info@lettrapress.com
www.lettrapress.com

Contents

Dedication vii
Special Dedication (overcoming all odds) vii

Introduction xi
"Sing Your Daddy's Song" 1
"Did You Ever Notice" 2
"Thoughtless" 3
"The Drunkenness Of Love" 4
"Love's Weakest Link" 6
"Good Book" 7
"A Cindy Sonnet" 9
"Referral Lovers" 10
"Between True Loves" 11
Thoughts of the night 12
"A Micky Overdose" 13
"The One That Got away" 14
"The One That Left In 64" 16
another midnight mumbler 18
"The Comings Of Around" 22
"Betrayed By The Rose" 24
"Here's to you baby" 26
"Everlasting Life"!!! 27
"Donaldson Run" 28
"Love--Infection" 30
"I Almost Miss The Pain" 31
"Misty Memory's" 32
"If I Had It All To Do Over" 34
"One Wife" 35
"In The Beginning" 37
"Dark Side Of My Heart" 38
"Moments Of Adoration" 39
"Memory's" 40
"Good Dreams" 43
*****"A Cindy Sonnet" #2***** 44
"Brooklyn Heights" 47

"Tonight My Pencil Will Be My Friend" 49
"So Tired" 51
"Back When" 52
"Crossing That "Ole" Bridge" 53
?? Maybe for all?? 54
{midnight memory mumbling 56
"I'm Paying Now" 57
"A Prince's sonnet" 59
"Hey Obama",[it ain't working] 60
"An Early-Morning Memory Row" 65
"My Bloomingdale's Lady" 66
Another Day – Another Time" 68
"I Still Dream About You" 69
"Never Again" 72
"I'll Take You, Lonely Or Not" 73
"Hockey – Tonk State Of Mind" 74
"A $54 Loan" 75
"Talk To Me Baby" 76
"My Sweet Little Indian Girl" 77
"Slow Drinking – No Thinking" 79
"Take Me Back Mama" 81
"Lie To Me" 83
"Get Ready" #1 85
"Donna I Don't Wanna" 88
"Gonna Drink Up All The Beer #1" 91
"Get Ready #2" 94
"Don't Tell Me Something I Already Know" 95
"The Boy Wearing Black" 97
"Red Vette Blues –#2" 99
"Honky-Tonk Heaven" 103
"The Blues Must Be Bluer Than Blue" 106
"The Mean "Ole" Cleanup Kitchen Blues" 108
"No Worries" 110
"Wastin' Time" 111
"I've Had Enough Of Your Mental Pain" 113
"Sing Your Daddy's Song" 115
"Slipping way" 116
"Take It Round The World" 117

Dedication

Volume #3 of Poems – songs and Letters by "Vance" is dedicated with the same respect, and thoughts of the previous volumes. That would be, to all the people who played a part in providing me with a topic to write about, or gave me reason for writing. Their names are very important to me, but need not be disclosed. They will know who they are, if or when they read it.

Special Dedication (overcoming all odds)

I believe it is pretty well-known to everybody, especially our relatives, that I am Teddy's, or Ted's if you prefer, older brother. In the past year I have gotten to know Ted for the man he has worked so hard to become. He has, from time to time overcome what most people would consider insurmountable odds. A mountain too high to climb, or a load too heavy to carry. But I can personally guarantee that thought would never ever enter Teddy's mind. If you were to show Ted an impossible situation, either in life or in business, he will show you just how quickly he can conquer it. Ted has a – "Can-Do" attitude.
/can't\ is not in his vocabulary!
The inherit ability to overcome. The intestinal fortitude that allows one to reach way down to the innermost hiding places of your soul, and in your mind, to succeed. Because to people like Teddy, success is what it's all about. Whether it be personal or business, it's all the same trip. And Ted, has had quite a trip, and while taking that trip, allowed some of us to ride along. Just from the little parts that I know about, it has been a very interesting ride, to say the least.
[in the beginning]
putting my mind in memory mode is something I enjoy doing. And the nice thing about memories is you can choose the ones you want

to deal with. The first time I have a memory of Teddy was when I was about five years old. From that point in my life until I graduated from high school, I would make an appearance about every year for as long as two weeks to two months. I shared a lot of good times and good memories, with not just Ted, but the rest of the family as well.

We lived close the railroad and the road so we could take our pick, hitchhike or hop a train. I never hopped a train, but I imagine Teddy did. Coming through those times as I recall, Teddy's biggest problem area was his inability to say yes or no and agree when necessary. While not being able to do so would innovatively administer his stubborn – bullheaded – never give up ways.

A lot of us have those ways, but Ted's was just always a little bit over the top. And sometimes it did not work out to his benefit.

I remember picnic's, reunions, hayfields, a summer vacation to Florida.
I daresay, through the springtime of our lives,
Teddy got in trouble more than anybody else.

Sometimes it kind of seemed like he enjoyed it. But I believe it was because he was born with his own agenda. It did not matter what anybody else said or wanted to do, Ted was going to do what Ted wanted to do. As a young man, he voluntarily joined the United States Marine Corps, where he served a four-year stretch.

And so began the structuring for the summertime of his life. Which by the way, remains true to form and intact to this day.

I would hear about his motorcycle and dirt – bike, hill climbing days. The race cars, or some of the incidents occurring in whatever business he was doing. It just gave you the idea that he was going to keep coming back for more. Ted lost his right hand while working on a dozer. He heals up, gets a hook and goes on to become one of the best crossbow artists in the world. Holding titles in both state and national championships

Then one very windy day
while Ted was hard at play
a rather large tree got in his way

he had looked but nothing in sight
then suddenly in his line of flight
it introduced him to a dreary night

hell, only 16 breaks on one leg
is that all you got to make me pay
I'll be back to slice you up some day
and so it goes!!!

When I look back to when he tried to cut a tree down
with his plane and broke his leg and 16 places.
And before he's even completely healed he gets another plane.
Man, I just don't know where the hell you are coming from.
I get a bunion on my toe and it damn near renders me useless.
Plus, you shoot a real mean game of pool, and a hot hand of poker.
It is always my pleasure losing to you and your two very fine sons,
Timmy and Tommy.
Ted, you are certainly, by far and above worthy of the dedication of this
book. As I look back over the things I've heard and seen about your life,
not only are you "one of a kind", but you are also a very good teacher.
You taught me that I would be
so much better off with broken hearts, and
a miseried mind, than an overdose of broken bones.
And I still wish we could have been partners in business. I know we
would have been a success.
Because you are always right, and I am always right,
and 2 rights, don't make a wrong!!!

Teddy's name would always come up out of reverence or fear.
So much so, the resemblance of basic makeup and tenacity,
to say nothing of his appearance, makes it obvious to people that don't
even know him, who his father was.
I am sure that makes Ted very happy. I think we all would like to be a
little more like dad, whether we admit it or not.

"This Songs for you Teddy"

You sang your daddy's song –
Ted you sang your daddy's song

you didn't cry when life slipped out of place
you put it back where it belonged

you solved all life's problems
right straight from the heart

with the mind control to never
let another problem start

yes, you sang your daddy's song –
Ted you sang your daddy's song!!!

"God" Bless Ya Ted – I Love Ya Man"
Brother – Keith

Introduction

The poems songs and letters described and written
in this, the "Sing Your Daddy's Song" volume by Vance,
refer to people, places, or events either experienced
by or known to the author. All accountings are true.
Some, however, may be
blessed with flavor, and color, or flair, if you will.
Those will be left to the individual readers interpretation
or discretion. There has been no intent
o mislead or wrongly inform during the assembling of this volume.

Please keep in mind, a writer cannot squash
that which flows from mind to paper.
Neither imagination or integrity will permit.

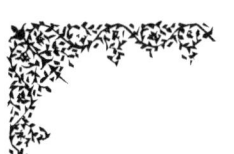

"Sing Your Daddy's Song"

[from the 70s]

Sing your daddy's song – son
sing each line with a smile

you know he lived it all – boy
and he made it all worthwhile

although you may wonder
and sometimes make a blunder

just sing it loud
and sing it proud
your living out his plan

don't think about where you're going
cause you have no way of knowing
you're an extension, of your daddy's hand

You sang your daddy's song – Ted
you sang your daddy's song

you didn't cry when life slipped out of place
you put it back where it belonged

you solved all life's problems
right straight from the heart
with the mind control to never
let another problem start

yes, you sang your daddy's song – Ted
you sang your daddy's song!!!

"Did You Ever Notice"
[rewritten—8-7-2013]
by
Roberta (Vance) Phillips & Keith Vance

see how the ground of the forest comes in line
with fallen leaves woven by needles of the pine
oh, did you ever notice
the conversations of the forest families
are greeted by the whispering leaves
as they find their place of rest so sure
while constructing nature's velvet floors
[chorus]
did you ever notice, the whole beauty of creation
now – did you ever notice – the trees and the grass
the ground, the water, and the stars are all relation
did you ever notice – oh – did you ever notice

****

the sound of trickling water – from rocks to creek
beds edge
comes in harmony with heaven – as it tucks the stars in bed
oh – did you ever notice
as sure as night gives up to light
another day is close at hand
a simple clear reminder
it's a part of "God's" great plan
o-o-o-h – did you ever notice
[end with chorus]
did you ever notice, the whole beauty of creation
now – did you ever notice – the trees and the grass
the ground, the water, and the stars are all relation
did you ever notice – oh – did you ever notice???

Although I have had no comments as to yea or nay
I can only hope we have done justice to the private
thoughts of Janice E. (Liller) Judy.

"Thoughtless"
5-16-1960 – through 5-16-2010

though I am blessed with love so fine
still, life with me is hard sometimes
not one can stand the life I live
I take from all but naught I give
he who treats his own two hands
must surely be a lesser man
to pluck a bush of roses bare
is truly a selfish act of care
to take from where the beauty rests
and concede to none of life's true tests
as ego soars when accolades mount
with achievements no one can count
who catches a star as it begins to fall
how lonely be the bottom, when it calls!!!

"The Drunkenness Of Love"
5-16-2016

I live my life as one man
out of control and with no plan
to escape the drunkenness of love
which all my life I have been a victim of
love has left me in the most drunken state of mind
kept me dreaming, kept me searching
for the everlasting kind
always returning to the yester time
when such a love was truly mine
now, without body, without label
I find myself unable
to stabilize the mentalness
necessary to assess
from whence cometh that sweet caress
which flows from love and drunkenness
both wine and women play a part
one of the head, one of the heart
wine is consumed without reason
women are never out of season
having more of both then I deserve
I feel I'm trapped in life's best curve
with no solution near at hand
nor desire to be a lesser man
I find myself in full caress
of what might be my final mess
enjoying pleasures of unconsciousness
thrilled by unmeasured happiness
loved by women, numbed by wine
'tis a true wonder of all time
to differ from this life of mine
would truly be, my end of time!!!

[Excerpt from volume 1]

my weakness is women, they do strange things to
me
though they're all the same, each one is different
you see
my only trouble is, I love them all the same way
when my weakness set in, it came to stay
to be true to one, it could never ever be
always on the run, it's the weakness in me
please don't hold it against me, for what I've said
or done
because I know when you're smiling, my heart's
having fun!!!

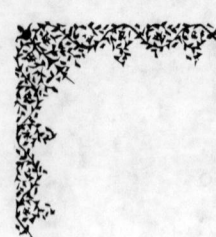

"Love's Weakest Link"
8-15-1967

it's not that you don't love me
instead, 'tis my love that is gone

I was never one for misery
so I'll just be moving on

you will think back and realize
as I have done before

a spark stays hot but to disguise
the flame that burns no more

to another, someday you will say
much like I have said to you

as they desire your pleasing ways
but your love cannot be true

then I, in a yester-memory, make you think
in our chain of love, mine was the weakest link!!!

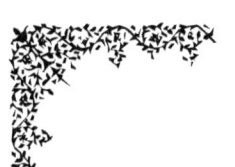

"Good Book"

10-10-2010

[song]

you're like a good book baby
I love to read you through and through

you got lots of blank pages
and honey I don't need you

now I'm going to tell you something
you might not – a – thought about

I got along good with you
and I can get along without

baby you left the best deal
that you will ever know

It'll be dancing in your memory's
no matter where you go

you know I hate to say it baby
but there is nothing left of you

you're as empty as my pockets
is my message getting through

you're personality is artificial
with an undercover fantasy

I really can't find a way to say
I'm glad you shared it with me

yeah, you're a good book baby
with the phony cover, just like you

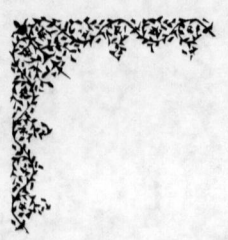

with pages good for toilet paper
that's the only way you ever knew

aw, but you're a good book baby
I like a good book now and then

a little fictions good, for the heart, the mind
and the soul
when you're playing a game you can't win!!!

"A Cindy Sonnet"

[the original poem style]
11-20-2015

I have nothing left in me to give to you
empty of promises, which I have made a few

still, I will take all you have for me
not because you give, but of my hearts thievery

your heart lives in a world of make-believe
while my heart is filled with pure deceit

oh my dear, how I wish it were not true
a special sadness one can feel, I will share with you

to need someone you cannot have
your final deal to save

from day one when we first met
I have thoughts of nothing less

just to hold you near, would be my next request
enter a love of visual lust, you, will be my guest!!!

Reasons you should consider
I wish I had met you earlier in life. I know
we could have a lot of fun. One thing I know
for sure, you would never have been treated
the way you were if I had been the one.
I will refer you to the previous lines
they should explained just how I feel
then leave it up to you to determine
if what I say is real.

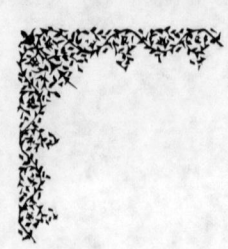

"Referral Lovers"

7-26-1973

I recall times I shared with lovers
that had been sent to me by others

and that is, oh, so good to know
it helps control the way things go

making sure that she's not bored
means she will be back for more

find out what she likes, then do it
the way she likes, get right down to it

let her know her love is special
for her presence you are grateful

when her body quakes and her toes curl
and the magic moaning sounds unfurl

as her thoughts make words of love's release
you'll know for the reference, she was pleased!!!

"Between True Loves"

[mid to late 70s]

one or two and sometimes even three
much like the satire gods of Greece

love and satisfaction is what they took from me
without requiring hearts bequeath

for their desire to soon return
gave gratefulness my heart to burn

and hurry deep into loves pleasure
with desired performance above all measure

embedded deeply in my mind, were memories of yore
of many one time lovers, but then returned no
more
so with concentration I became more mentally aware
to fill all needs and pleasure's of those put to my care
my inter-thoughts grew only to bring them happiness
upon success I found my own hidden world of
bliss
as my confidence built, so too did my content
in knowing, a true love for me, was never meant!!!

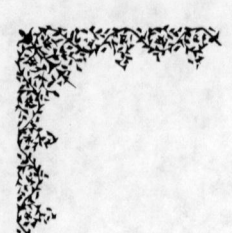

Thoughts of the night
3-28-92

as I look around the room
I see all these pictures of you

but there is no sign of gloom
you had the world by the ass

"God" gave everything to you
and all you did was let it pass

you enjoyed living high on life
believing there would be no strife

of one thing you were very sure
for all your needs, "God" would procure

you never thought or wondered why
life seemed so easy to get by

you partook of all He passed your way
and all you had to do was pray

you knew there'd never come a time
when you would surpass His limit line

nor did you even think of such
because you knew, He loves you much

He always comes through in a clutch
that, tells you you're not out of touch
thank you "God"!!!

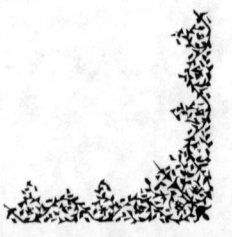

"A Micky Overdose"

4-3-16

my little Micky, I have consumed thee twice
all be your flavor, extremely nice

as I ponder, should of thee, I partake more
oh yes, please permit, all I can endure
"you're a sweetheart"
not one compares with the sweetness you exude
whilst my desire is your contentment to include

could we make this a never ending night
one that sets intimacies in full flight
and liberates the feeling's you hide with might

just knowing your heart blossoms does pleasure bring
to have, hear, and hold, the sounds of your heart strings
brings a sweet resolve to the lust, of which my heart sings

to have my fill of you Micky, I have not come close
so I shall consume you, until I dream an overdose!!!

"The One That Got away"
{date unknown}

"Everybody talks about the one that got away.
I wrote this piece for a very special young lady,
she will know it's for her. I do not feel it necessary to
divulge the name. However, as I look back over
my life, I feel it should have been written by me

many-many years ago. It seems that for one reason
or another, they all got away. Including my darling,
love of my life, wife. Obviously it must have been
from failure on my behalf, to do or not to do. It
certainly was not their fault. They were all very
special, and I honor them the way they honored
me. To the very best of my ability, from mental
notes, memoirs, and songs I wrote for them"!!!

Insert from volume 1
though my title fails her sorely
this lady fills that bill

I miss her so adoringly
her pleasures haunt me still

to quote the friends that envied me
"you should have imposed your will"

with respect of her desire for chastity
by her pleasured company I was thrilled

and so my memory's yield a glowing
while I watch her body sway

with complete content of knowing
as through my dreams we play

she no longer lives in haunting
for she's the one, that got away!!!

"The One That Left In 64"
6-26-68

the one that left in 64
left my heart broken
and my mind sore

I filtered through unwanted loves
with a life not worth dreaming of

four long years, then from above
came what was to be a lasting love

to a life of love's, a mangled mess
came one who put my mind at rest

there could not have been a better time
to engage a person so sublime

she lifted me to heights unknown
heights I knew were not my own

these heights were hers, instilled in me
she gave me strength and victory

without our meeting just by chance
life would have been a different dance

most likely with the stage procured
from lust-filled feelings unsecured

instead, "God" was looking down
and heard a life of worthless sounds

a life for which He had proclaimed success
yet chooses to settle for anything less

with control of all His discontent
He calmly arranged a settlement

one He knew that I could handle
one He knew was not a gamble

with beauty I could not ignore
to heal one heart left so sore

He brought a lady by my side
He knew I would choose to be my bride

I have always thanked Him for the intervention
it meant much more than I could mention

in my life "God" has always played a part
I think because He knows my heart

He always provides me with my needs
and in spite of myself makes me succeed

this time he brought new meaning to my life
and introduced me to my darling wife

all the pleasures of life I could afford
could not compare, with my love for the Lord

he calmed the storms for ever more
and erased all pains from 64!!!

another midnight mumbler

why???
Sometime between 1942
and 2017-mostly-3-28-88

did you ever take the time
just to listen to your mind
one should take the time
to listen to one's mind
one side says stop
the other side says go
one side says fast, the other side says slow
one side says yes, the other side says no
one might be surprised at what one finds
or one might realize to reality one is blind
I just laid down and began to wonder
who of importance would know
who's important
who cares who knows
I suppose that's why we can't lay down
just to lay down and die
we keep pushing to go
I will go until my body won't permit
when it no longer permits, I'll still go
until my mind does not permit
and if my mind does not permit
I'll fight that too
oh, just for the record
I am a Washington Redskin fan
ridiculed though they may be
by governmental PC
they will survive the ridiculous rhetoric
and the bull-shit lies

of whatever government official
tries to lay claim to our tribes
they will win another Super Bowl soon
and on that day, Sitting Bull
will rise from the dead to publicly expose
the narrow minded one-way thinking
of the aforementioned official, and sports analysts,
for just what they are, and while doing so
Sitting Bull, will sit on their bull-shit
charges and accusation, they need to get a life
and the only thing I will miss about this event
would be the lovemaking session, of choice,
with my all time favorite love maker
and Redskin fan
De'dr, where do ye be?
Come to me in memory
for one last Redskin victory
Although we will watch this event together – apart
we will, as always, be together in our hearts!
what a bunch of crap
life goes on, time goes by
shit rolls downhill, and birds fly
a way up high away from it
because they're smarter than us
and that ain't no shit
the muscles of time tighten around my heart
with strangling strength that makes me start
to choke on what has kept us apart
we had a love to pure to the end
still in the end we could not blend
because of time, life's adversary
always erupting the unnecessary

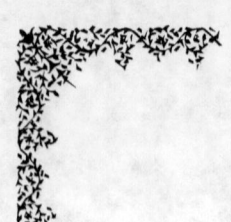

things we didn't need to hear
things we did not need to know
things that would surely cause us weer
things that cause love not to grow
the stifling sounds of idle chatter
will hurt the heart and sometimes shatter
the hopes and dreams we hold so close
with those we love and cherish most
I know they'll never be another you
you know they'll never be another me
for all those years we loved so true
remains inclusive, as love should be
why???
Your love for me grows
my love for you grows
yet, our love dies
I drink to you
you are my very special Angel
why why why
is it just so screwed up
the thought of you still takes my breath away
then permits me to return and live another day
so – o –o bad here without you Dee Dee!!!

*****

prepare yourself for the comings of around
they usually attack without making a sound
understanding why, can sometimes be hard
and when it is all over your heart is charred

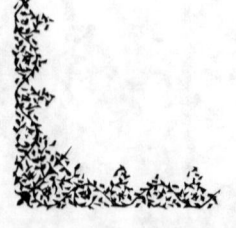
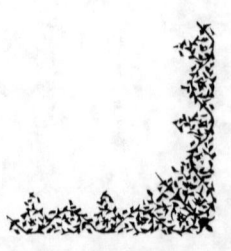

{thoughts of 66 through 87}

[song]
I think I'll go inside
and have a bowl of misery

go inside, and take a shot of pain relief
go inside and baby, set your memory free

I'm gonna drown my brain and try to refrain
from believing what has happened to me

yes I'll have the kind of misery
that I can chase with a glass of pain

I don't know how many memory's i've made
total recall drives me insane

I know I've made a bunch with you
that I can hold close to my heart

those memories will pay my dues
for the price life has charged

I have an overdose of pain and misery
it's going to take a big shot of pain relief
to finally set me free!!!

"The Comings Of Around"
[from the 80s]

what goes around, comes around
you hear it all the time

this time baby, it will be your turn
you've already, delivered mine

what goes around, comes around
I believe it must be true

or I can still remember
when I was not missing you

though strange it may seem
it all changed with a dream
now I'm wanting you back

but I know that can't be
time turned the tables on me
still, your love is the one thing I lack

the time will come when you will feel the same
you'll want me back but you can't bear the shame

the shame of too much pride to allow my return
then like me, in your heart a scorching fire will burn

the heat of the fire will be so intense
it will melt the mending of any fence

then you'll realize just how much I missed you
when true love dies, there is nothing you can do!!!

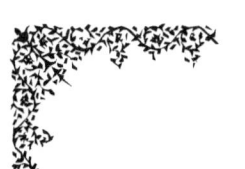

[thoughts from 89]
a beautiful bright sunshiny morning
my thoughts of you gave no warning
immediately sends me to
a semi-stable state of mourning
this cannot go on, for you are gone
and this, I must realize
or accept your loss, as my demise

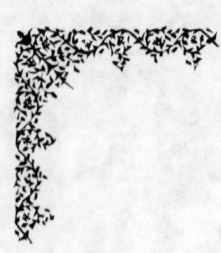

"Betrayed By The Rose"
5-16-1973

oh – they think that I don't know
my love is gone, still left – a Rose

a Rose that I once bought for her
but then, her love became a blur

not understood, without command
still it seemed our love would stand

the perils of time, as one love goes
now you are gone, remains the Rose

as tears fall, from heart to ground
a flood of petals all around

our love was fine as good loves go
but I have been betrayed, by the Rose

a Rose that I once held so near
the Rose I held, was you my dear

I plucked a blossom and watched it grow
into betrayal, by the Rose

now you are gone, the Rose has died
I'm left alone, to pay loves price

an unhealthy price, as we all know
brings our life's chapter, to a close

as your love dies, so goes the Rose
but remains forever, in sweet repose
never shall I hold

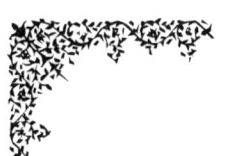

another one like you,
neither
heart, mind, nor soul
doth, want to
yes, our love was great, as great loves go
now I find my heart betrayed, by the Rose

I truly picked you as a blossom
then watched you grow into a flower

only to be stolen away
by a lustful, late – night coward

oh I never want the reason
and, I never care to know

why I have been betrayed
by life's only – worthy Rose!!!

"Here's to you baby"

those who succumb to the hands of thieves
as life's gifts pass, are only left to grieve!!!

[The deliverance of time]

I could write a book about this story of the "Rose"
though some may wonder why
instilled in me – it has become
the one true love – that will not die
life has been so good to me
I have lived a life that most men – can only dream about
but then, there is a reverse side to that
most men
have a life – that I – can only dream about !!!

I write it the way I lived it, and I lived it believing in "God,"
and myself, the way, I wanted to!
One day you have it all, the next day you have nothing.
When you think you have nothing,
others think you have it all
And so the cycle continues, you strive to achieve
what you consider all. Yet, somehow, you
do the same to have nothing
During this same process you secure your nothing
Place
then it all begins again.
And so, with eyes, heart, and mind open,
you reach for the new and start over
this process has been a regular part of my life. I have
climbed more ladders, slid down more fire escapes,
than most firemen. Still, I continue to follow a dream.
It may not be the first dream I ever had, since I am a man
of many dreams and goals. Which, is a characteristic that I

shall continue to include in my basic makeup. On the day I cross over the great divide to my next life and new home, with Jesus Christ, our heavenly father, I will still be looking onward and upward to my newest, and proudest of, dreams and the goals. I plan on being around for a long time, even after I am gone. For I have been given the promise, of an

"Everlasting Life"!!!
[A sonnetorial response to political comments]
3-14-16

I have always liked and respected Charles Krauthammer
until he became a Trump slammer

it appeared to be without reason
except what Trump said wasn't pleasing

to the one-way ears of this analyst
so he responded as he thought best

if he were not so in to planting judgment seeds
perhaps his comments would have served a need

while at the start many minds were empty
to the flourishing of a Trump-ness plenty

I would ask, where would we be
without these acts in history

when we provided a response to the blame
and were met with anger to disown the shame!!!

"Donaldson Run"
10-18-1988

well I used to walk to Roslyn
and drop a card to you

then I'd trip around to Cherrydale
to let our love slip through

with memories of things we've done
while having so much fun

and sometimes on holidays
I would drop by Donaldson Run

I remember all the pets we had
and everything you said

all the promises we made
and the poetry we read

while lying on the grass
together, we became one

those memories are always here
when I visit Donaldson Run

with Christmas fast approaching
it's harder now than before

memories of moments spent
in loving times of yore

I just can't kick the feeling dear
of your loving tender touch

and the plans we prematurely made
when love meant more than much

I never lost that loving feeling
that, I will hold for you

it has a home inside my heart
until my life is through

but now I'm getting older
as are the times for having fun

they have passed me by, as I recall
the days of Donaldson Run

oh my dear darling Donna
though we are now apart

you should know without me saying
never will another have my heart

forever, is a lifetime with you
on beaches in the sun

while in my mind, in memory
I return to Donaldson Run!!!
love you baby

[thoughts from the 70s – late 80s and early 90s]

"Love--Infection"

well it seems my life has been in full rejection
or maybe, total rejection from me
I have left myself open to reception
while searching for an infectious disease
one I never tried to guard against
but quite invisible it be
'tis a disease of the heart, mind, and soul
and inflicts nothing, but misery
one I did not solicit
it appears very nonchalantly
there is no scientific cure
no medicine or known remedy
when it strikes it fits your body like a glove
by now you figured out, this infection is called love!!!

"I Almost Miss The Pain"
3-28-97

oh I'll take away the tears
you have taught me how to cry

and I'll take away the times
I used to sit and wonder why

and I'll read the words on cards
and letters I have here

while I'm trying to console
a heart that's filled with fear

but it's getting to the point
that I almost miss the pain

I've grown so used to being hurt
please, do that again

the other day I mashed my thumb
and later realized it hurt

when from beneath my fingernail
the blood began to squirt

I guess I need another broken heart
for physical refrain

yes, it's getting to the point
that I almost miss the pain

won't you please come back and promise to remain
so when you decide to leave I can almost go insane

please have pity on me honey, and lie to me again
for it's getting to the point, I almost miss the pain!!!

"Misty Memory's"
11-29-72

oh I can taste those misty morning's
followed by each sunrise at dawn

as I relive our yester-years
and the love we had going on

the good times we had together
blessed the memory's of it all

yes I miss you more as the days go by
and sunrise yields to a misty morning call

oh, I think back to how sad I felt
when you told me we would never love again

I could not believe if "God" was just
the life I lead be allowed to bust
apart, the sweetest love He would ever send

as the tears of misty sorrow tips my tongue
each morning as the sun gives up its youth
as the day winds down, begins to tell the truth
showing distance between now
and when our love was young

so deep, true, and honest, our love did feel
surpassed the norm of tenderness, uncovering our wild
from our hearts we drew the power of passion
to perform our obsessive dreams with zeal
sometimes revealing immature experiments
one could only think of as a child

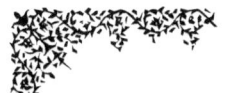

I shall never know those times again
you have brought them to an end

now, you are gone, but mentally I replay
that part of my life with you will always stay

over and over, recording in my mind
the truest love that I would ever find

and so I taste the misty memory's, of our last nights love
midst tears of tenderness, flowing freely on my tongue
abandoning me with only yearnings of
times we knew and loved, when we were young!!!

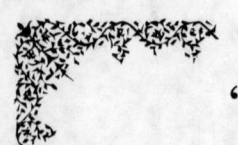

"If I Had It All To Do Over"
11-29-72
[song]

chorus
well if I had it all to do over
I'd do the same damn thing with you

I liked every one of the things we've done
I'd like to do-em again, it was fun

oh, if I had it all to do over
I'd do the same damn thing with you

a-lot-a people don't believe me
but honey, I swear it's the truth

if I had it all to do over
I'd do the same damn thing with you
yes I'd do it all over with you!!!

****

"One Wife"
11-29-2002

someone told me one time
that I should never take a wife

that I probably should live single
for the rest of my life

that I had a way about me to repel all trust
a wanderers look, with wanting ways of lust

I suppose I should have listened
for here I am alone

but I came in as a single
and that's the way I'll take it home

still I've had lots of lovers
to help me through the perils of life

with a few commitments of betrothal
but I have only had, one wife!!!
{unconscious midnight mumbling}
hyperbole, yes hyperbole – is a word, dumb ass
you will find the meaning in the looking glass
if you see yourself and hold your place
the end of an era you will erase
but if you choose not to look into the deep
it tells not the time of life that's cheap
oh, the lack of luster one must feel
when genius trumps what's really real
is there no excitement to your charge
when all life's pleasures are at large
denial must be, cry me me to sleep
if all that's left is for you to weep

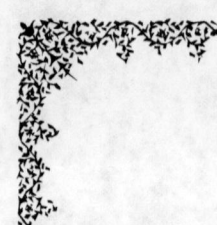

from here to for with nothing more
gives life one option, shut the door
but then your genius does explode
into a verbiage mother-load
and once again, you can proclaim
there is no fire without a flame
the flame that burns inside of me
the flame that will not set me free
the flame that fires the heart and soul
the flame that never lets me go
t's there, it's there no matter where
to go from here and then to there
without the questions of but where
who knows where it is all going
do you know for sure what you're doing
if I thought for one minute, that I knew
do you think I'd do the things I do
I have served life as a peasant slave
and wished for things I could not have
while knowing others that had flourished
left me feeling motherless and un – nourished
though contradiction fill the air
it may be time I should declare
the one that holds the heart and soul
is the one that truly has control
and I will happily confess
'tis the one that I love best
she gave my heart a whirl, she is my girl
from now to after-life, she, is my world!!!

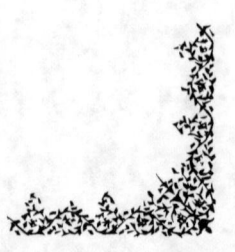

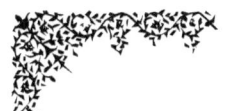

thoughts from the 60s]

"In The Beginning"

no concern had I when love got sidetracked in my youth
with numbers mounting, to reference such would be uncouth

as sure as dawn would break to bring the light of day
they came to take my love and steal my heart away

with no defense for loves addiction
with each one came true perfection

acquainted ones would tread the steps of others
a friendly tongue, or satisfied remarks of lovers

still, I am indebted but to very few
the ones that gave me love so true

for the ones that came to play loves game
were without the spark that fans the flame

seeking satisfaction that compares
to one that climbed those empty stairs

so consequently, the pattern formed
to please the hearts, that needed warmed!!!

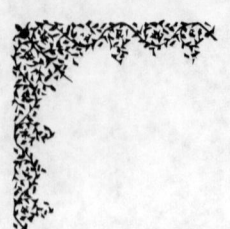

"Dark Side Of My Heart"
3-28-91

take another look at me darling
checkout the dark side of my heart

yeah, take a real good look
at what's coming back to get you
and tear your world all apart

now "God" let Delilah handle Sampson
in a way no man has ever known

she took away his strength
then "God" gave it back
and he tore down that house of stone

it was a nice surprise when I met you
one I was not searching for

Oh, you said I love you true
no one else will ever do
then you walked out and slammed the door

so take another look at me baby
take a look at the dark side of my heart

take a good long look
at what's coming back to get you
and tear your world all apart!!!

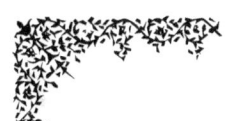

"Moments Of Adoration"

1-12-1990
unfinished
[it may never be able to be finished]

I have read Poe, Frost, Dylan,
Shakespeare, and Michelangelo
they were all the geniuses.
still, I find none more consoling than my own.
which I suppose, is as it should be!!!

"Memory's"
(5-16-2002—my 60th)

living on memory's
memory's that last
memory's of my fortune's
memory's of my past
memory's of my failures
and I've had a few
but mostly darlings
fond memory's from all of you
I've got a steady diet
of misery and pain
that's what keeps me alive
it's food for my brain
I don't have much to live for
except a new memory each day
but I have had a full life
in so many, many way's
somehow I keep dreaming
of a whole different life
and my most special memories
were made with my wife
still, I am never lonesome
and I like it that way
those "ole" blues never find me
for I was born to play
yes, play a part of a loser
in this game called life
yet I've never been lost
just consumed by strife
my hearts never empty
instead, it's overflowing
with memory's of good times
that completes me by knowing
nothing was wasted

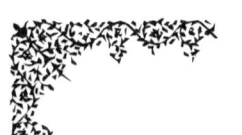

or thrown away
and when it's all over
it will be a happy day
so I'll just keep on dreaming
as I have always done
and as life's corners turn
I will dream another one Yes, another memory
to take with me
and oh, what a memory
more fuel for my run
that's what I've always done
for that's what I live on
it keeps my life fun
and memory's are the givers of fun
"and I live for fun"!!!

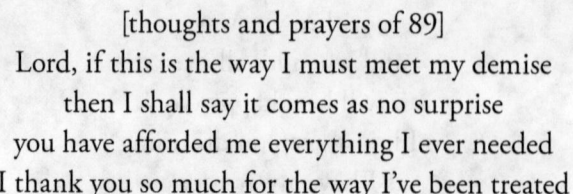

[thoughts and prayers of 89]
Lord, if this is the way I must meet my demise
then I shall say it comes as no surprise
you have afforded me everything I ever needed
I thank you so much for the way I've been treated

I hope I've been forgiven of all my sins
my short – comings I will try to amend
if this is the way I must go out, let it be a
warning for others, so they do not meet the
same fate. After living the life I have lived,
I love you "God", and I drink to my life and
the way I have lived it with your help.
Thank you again!!!

may all the people I have befriended along
the way, be blessed. I hope they enjoyed the
time we had to spend together. I love them all,
friends, family, and lovers!!!

the end is not the end, but the beginning. I look
to you for my reward. My mansion, and the
streets of gold that you have prepared for me.
"God", have mercy on me and help me, I have
so much more that I must do.
sleep is a wonderful thing, please let me do so!!!

"Good Dreams"
[11-29-2016]

the nice thing about my dreams
is they are all about you

yes the nice thing about my dreams
you always say everything I want you to

you're so quick to step up and protect my heart
you drive away the memories that tore us apart

the nice thing about my dreams
is that I am in control

and as long as I'm dreaming
you play the main role

oh, the nice thing about my dreams
is I am never alone

you slip in at midnight
and stay until dawn

we say night things and play night games
just like we used to do

yes, the nice thing about my dreams
is they are all about you!!!

*****"A Cindy Sonnet" #2*****
{reworked to another sonnet format}
5-30-16
2:15 a.m.

I have depleted on you, many brain cells
for reasons I don't know, or can not tell
I can only hope these words on paper
will provide pleasure, filled with laughter

*****

I have nothing left in me to give to thee
empty of promises, which I have made a few
not because you give, but of my life's view
I will take all that you have for me

your heart lives in a world of make-believe
while my heart is filled with limits to be true
the special sadness I feel, to know I can't have you
oh my dear, how I pray you do not receive

to need someone you can't retrieve
your final deal to prove
when we met, youthful thoughts began anew
but not, to hold you near, then take my leave

instead, to give you all you would receive
enter a love of visual lust, and live in my fantasy!!!

Reasons you should not consider
I have had much more happiness in life than I deserve
and it seems that I find more after every curve

I take from those I love without intending
not of monetary value, but that of mental bending

down through the years I have been first
drilled that way as a child
"you must never settle for anything less
lest it cramps your style"
so I took the best life had to offer
now, here I am alone
and once again I find myself
searching for a reason to atone
the love you have to give, is worthy of possessing
don't deal it out to someone you'll end up regretting
you have been a friend since our first sight
which lends credence to the way I've lived my life
I have been gifted with the knowing
of a meeting just by chance
then left behind a trail of love's
and deeply disappointed feelings of romance
to say nothing of the distance in our ages
staying true to the way I've turned life's pages
I would not damage your finances
though your mind would never be the same
as I make an attempt to prove myself
capable of pursuing one last game
consider all I have confessed to you
then to your own heart be true
and whatever your decision be
I am pleased and pleasured, knowing thee!!!

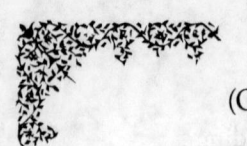

(Oh, by the way, one more word to the wise)
take what you will from the message
these lines have spoken
my mother once told me
"promises to you are like eggs
they are made to be broken"

[Wisdom is golden]
do not let poets words of rambling
cause you to take up gambling
just remember words are cheap
and we, with dictionaries, only weep!!!

"Brooklyn Heights"
7-23-16

I've got 14 pieces of barn board
that came out of Brooklyn Heights

and if these boards could talk
they could tell stories all night

well – a – way back when
the "ole" saw – mill towns were in

ladies of the night, from Brooklyn Heights
let men know they were men

filled with bullet holes and bloodstains
these "ole" boards have a history

now some might lie or try to hide
it was a well-known mystery

no – one went home unsatisfied
and if they tried, they died

by the hand of Brooklyn Heights pride
Pecker – Wood Security was on their side

it was the custom for the ladies just to say maybe
until they got their hands on your wallet

and if you had more than 10
it didn't matter where or when
whatever you wanted, you could call it

up against the wall, or out in the hall
in the bathroom, or the kitchen sink

they'd never tell you no
or wouldn't let you go
without a double shot of pink

you dropped your pants somewhere with Fancy
now it's around the world and back again

for another five they'd bring you back to life
you'd be praying that the night would never end!!!

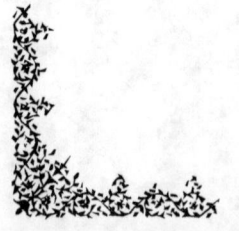

"Tonight My Pencil Will Be My Friend"
9-5-2016

tonight my pencil will be my friend
portraying memories without end
from youthful days when love begins
through all the days that love has been
from the tender innocence of youth
when all happenings surrendered truth
when good or bad required no proof
one could partake of all life's fruits
times when hate knew no morrow
when true love was not just to borrow

instead, would last through all tomorrows
while yielding happiness, free of sorrow
oh, I beg, tonight pencil, be my friend
write down the way this all should end
right my wrongs to make amends
do not allow my mind to bend
tonight pencil, please be my friend
take me from the times of love and laughter
all through the times of ever after
including all my thoughts or canters
show me the fruits of all I've planted
from the very few loves that knew no end
to all the ones which were but friends
from the loves I lost to the loves I'd win
let this not be to my chagrin
let this not be a saddening time
of someone searching for a rhyme
with little left that's really mine
life's honesty becomes sublime
hear me now pencil, when I say

carry me through the days of play
rescue me from life's disarray
to a final peace were I might stay
so pencil, once again I do implore
pull from the memory's of which you're sure
don't exaggerate to make it more
the truth shall be my final cure
so tonight pencil, be my friend
and bring this saga to an end!!!
Thank you

"So Tired"
3-28-82

I'm so tired of thinking every morning
    will this be the last day I see you

and I'm so tired of feeling that it's over
Lord knows, I'm so tired of being used

but I don't mind loves bruises darling
and I don't care about the broken heart

I don't care about a single thing dear
accept I'm so tired of us being apart

I'm so tired of thinking every evening
might be the last time I make love to you

and I'm tired of worrying about it darling
I guess I'm just damn tired of being blue

if you have it in your heart, satisfy my mind
then I will not have to be so tired, all the time!!!

{more from the house that Donna built}
"Back When"
3-28-88

it's a long long time from the dreams of day one
back when dreaming was always so much fun

you always wrapped our dreams with a lovers spin
back when a dreamer could do nothing but win

the way time has flown by is hard to conceive
leaving it all behind for the dreamer to weave

we had a love from above and we took our best shot
now dream woven memories are all that I've got

with you I took the last chance I had
you are the one dream that ended so sad

back when I moved mountains and you were my queen
I return there quite often to relive our dream

back when the new-ness of love uncovered its youth
when our time spent together knew nothing but truth

I think I'll send my mind, on an endless trip in time
when our dreams were full, and our love was so fine

it's the most comfortable place I can find
Back When You Were Mine!!!

****

You spin it your way, and I'll dream it mine
it's so nice to have a love, that will outlast time

****

"Crossing That "Ole" Bridge"
(winter- 1987)

just about the time I settle for a heartache
you come crawling back into my mind
and I'm crossing that "ole" Bay Bridge one more time
trying to drive you out of my mind
reliving the memory of all time
crossing that 'ole' bridge one more time
with memory's of love, a love that made us blind
includes the memory of a love that broke my mind
somewhere between O. C. and D. C.
I'll be crossing that "ole" bridge one more time
maybe that bridge will keep me from losing my mind
I remember that night outside of Fenwick
we pulled your car over by the Bay
"God" only knows where you learned how to play
but I believe we were both born that way
born to be lovers and satisfy each other
with no worries of where it takes place
these mental memory's helps keep me on my way
and gives birth to another game we used to play
as I watch the car behind me, in my mirror
weaving back and forth, on and off the road
stirs up another state of mind, in another time
as my mind returns to places we would go

oh, I love a good memory, especially ones of you
to days gone by, of all the hidden things we'd do

yes, I love those memories, and those very special times

I may write a book about, all those memories of mine
and I will thank you baby for treating me so kind

filling my life's pleasures by making love so fine
while I'm crossing that "ole" Bay Bridge, one more time!!!
Thank you baby

[from the 80s]
?? Maybe for all??

Thoughts from 88 and 89

oh I've loved you more
than I should have

and I've loved you much longer
then most men would have

too many times
I've been close to losing my mind

from the emptiness you feel
when there's something left behind

seems I've loved you more than a lifetime
and I'll love you when my time is through

I know one day that you will find
no one could ever love you like I do

this kind of love I guess is best left unknown
so it's probably better that you've left me alone

for you can't watch me cry, or sit and wonder why
you won't be here to hold me, as I bid this world goodbye

but I will love you as long as I'm breathing
yes I'll love you in my final resting place

the very last thing I will see, when they cover me
is the smile that spreads across your gorgeous face

oh, how I have loved you
I have loved you much more than I should have
I've loved you so much more than most men could have

no matter what you do, I will always love you
I have loved you, with a love so true
it's killing me baby, and I'm having a hard time kicking it
you are here for the duration!!!

[thoughts from 88, and the house that Donna built]

memory joggers
refreshing memories, looking at pictures of you
she wore white like an angel
waiting for a hug
with balloons everywhere
just waiting to make love
on a sheepskin rug

*****

{midnight memory mumbling
5-16-17

"oh the coming's of around"
yields an unhealthy sound
from your past it keeps in play
loving memories of yesterday
it leaves you holding what is gone
faltering from the fruitless things you've done
oh the pain, the agony, the suffering it imposes
much like a house of horror, that never closes
may "God" protect you all from that feeling
there is no cure, nor enough time for healing

"I'm Paying Now"
1973
[song]

I had a talk with the "big guy"
he said I'm going to tell you what

son, you know you've got to pay
for everything you've got

nd I'm paying now I
think I'm all paid out

when my debt is through
I'm coming back to you

oh – I'm paying now
but I don't know how

and I don't know why
guess I'll be paying until I die

and I'm paying now
Lord – I've paid a lot

yes I'm paying now – –ow – –ow
with everything I've got

but when it comes to you, I guess it's true
I'll be paying till my days are through

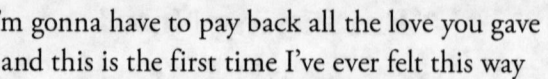

I'm gonna have to pay back all the love you gave
and this is the first time I've ever felt this way

the "big guy" said son, now you better behave
or you'll still be paying when you're in your grave

and I'm paying now – –ow – –ow
Lord I'm paying now

and when I get through I'm coming back to you
but I'm paying now!!!

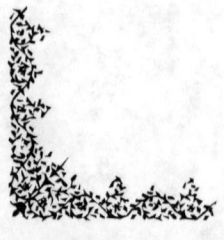

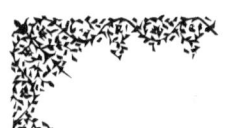

"A Prince's sonnet"

April 21, 2016
{the day the lure--became a Legend}

why do we all aspire in tearing down a dream
it took one man a life time to realize

with seemingly no respect for his unusual scheme
with no sense of the price he paid for his demise

the sleepless nights, the mental screams
he endured for our surprise

his every thought was for our happiness
to entertain us was his great love

yet for this love no fond caress
we only search for reasons of

if he took drugs, we taught him how---?
he had no life, we were his love

why can't we try to understand
he was a gift, from the great, "I AM"

"Hey Obama", [it ain't working]
2-20-2013

your health plan doesn't work
everyone I know thinks you're a jerk

thousands of pages of political BS
what it really says is anybody's guess

we could ask Pelosi, or maybe Harry Reid
but they are just like you, clueless indeed

now you say you want a drone
so you can spy on our own people

and you don't care if it passes
your executive privilege makes it legal

it ain't workin'
no Obama, that ain't working

now if golfing is your game
then maybe you will stay

you are so transparent
no one sees you anyway
it ain't workin'
no Obama, you ain't workin'
hey Obama
how about all those promises you made
did someone maybe tell you, promises were like eggs
I guess you made them to be broken
that's why everybody's jokin'

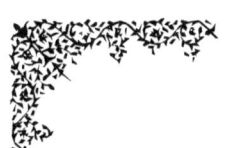

about "Obama Care", 1000's of pages
of insurance, for all ages

Obama care part one is out of gas
but Americans
are stupid, they will let it pass
but it ain't workin'
it's like cutting down a tree with a plain "ole" table knife
or like exercising options with your next-door neighbor's wife
[now that ain't workin']
it's like lying to our people cause the press will let it pass
it's like trying to mount a windshield
wiper on an elephant's ass
and you know damn well that ain't workin'

Hey Obama
you are such a nice guy, you don't know what to do
you tell so many lies even uncle Joe believes thier true
no more raising taxes, and everyone goes back to work
unemployment and food stamps make you look like a jerk
it ain't workin'
you're trying to pass a budget, but the Republicans won't play
they're just all against you, and they don't care what you say
it ain't workin'
it's like trying to cross the ocean on the boat with no gas
or like, you know, windshield wipers on an elephant's ass

(and we all know that ain't workin')

hey Obama, you got all this global knowledge
and you want the world to know
but "insane" Barack Obama
what you say don't make it so!

I will protect our borders, I'll put Iran back in its place
still you bow to the Muslim brotherhood
after 9/11 that is a disgrace!
and that ain't workin'

think about the country you represent
the next time you meet a Muslim leader

get your head out of the sand
stand up straight, and shake his hand!

Cause what you did, ain't workin'

you're always blaming other people
for handing you the past

I wonder who that elephant blames
for the windshield wipers on his ass
cause they ain't workin'
no they ain't workin, Obama, you ain't workin'!

maybe "ole" Rush was right
YOU JUST DON'T HAVE A CLUE!!!
Hey Obama
now you have been re-elected
although I sure as hell don't know how

but I bet it had something to do
with that "ole" Liberal – Cash – Cow

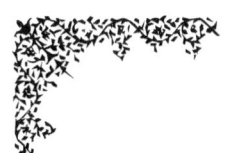

I would like to know the reasons
cause it's certainly not on merit

think of all our people you left hurting
and the "VETS", that could no longer bear it

think of all the broken promises you made
a new one almost every minute

your party will be rewarded for leading from behind
f you're lucky your eyes will be closed when you step in it

anyway, you were put back in office
one way or another

but you sure got it handed to you
by that little "doctor brother"

trying to pass all those gun bills
and getting rid of coal miners too

and now your courting Tiger
what will his women do???

When it comes to this sequester
keep your military fast

then, just maybe

you won't have to hear anymore
about that "ole" Elephant's Ass!!!

now that just ain't workin'
it's kinda like
leading from behind, or circle jerkin'
maybe community organizing was a good job for you
just think
since you've gone, what Chicago has gone through

maybe when you're out of office
you can glorify yourself

cause that is really not a task
you should assign to someone else

Only you know you are worthy
for the things you say you'll do

and you are sure to give yourself credit
but we all know it's not the truth

Barack Hussein Obama
retire, don't try to hang around
your popularity in America
is most certainly headed down!!!

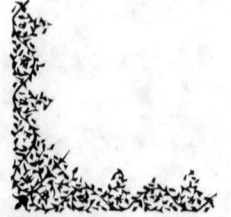

"An Early-Morning Memory Row"

7:00 AM
12-8-2016

awoken with the fondest recollection
brought about by the nights reflection

to that certain time in life
"God" blessed me with a wife

within her face a loving likeness
portraying beauty with all kindness

so soft the taunt of eloquence
left my heart with no defense

overwhelmed by love and laughter
and confident of happiness ever after

inside a web so gently woven
life projected such a glowing

the days, weeks, months, and years
with sudden smoothness disappears

granting distance to a wounded past
wrapped in the warmth of love at last

then came the dawn!
that uninvited dreadful dawn!

too soon displayed the truth in light
as a trip in time with dreams of night

leaves one in wanting just to know
why a mind that lives in afterglow
must take these trips down memory row!!!

"My Bloomingdale's Lady"
(late 70s)

she was a Bloomingdale's lady shopping at Zayre
I could not imagine what she was doing there

I said lady, my lady, you're a fine looking lass
what gives you misfortune to be under classed

she said life has been fun, life has been grand
but life does not always deal a good hand

as a matter of fact it's because of a man
you see me today the way that I am

without probable cause, I turned and then said
the man surely was daft, or soft in the head

to send you adrift would be so unkind
that thought should never enter one's mind

she looked back at me with invitational eyes
with an exhibition of elegance made her reply

words come so easy for those who don't know
but with timely persuasion love loses its glow

life's picture is a painting of everything roses
but most pictures lie, and everyone poses

we are not all the same, and no ones to blame
when we cannot succeed in loves crazy game

I have become quite calloused, in total control
determined to protect, my heart from the cold

but if you have a top-coat I could wear to my car
I shall return it to you, without leaving a scar

I took off my coat, and covered her shoulders
she kept her promise, while my desires smolder!!!

Another Day – Another Time"
1998

another day another time
when my desires were so defined
that in a heartbeat, became mine

when my age was not on trial
I'd waste no time to make you smile
then take my pleasures from your wild

nother time another day
so many more terms are now in play
which redirect desires and hold at bay

until the time to partake gives in
and prepares the hearts that I must win
with love – filled robust pleasures send

instead, the time and day is now
I am left with winters wrinkles on my brow
to only dream of, and wonder where or how

'twould be unfair to steal thy youth
and dare perform for you untruth
to imprison your happiness would be abuse

still, filled with dreams in my recent days
my heart desires to please its wanting ways
I fear I'll fail to treat you well, so I must walk away!!!

"I Still Dream About You"

[70s]

oh welcome back memory's, and welcome back love
you've been gone so long now, but I'm still thinking of

all of the good times, we had in the past
now maybe this time, our love will last

so give it your best shot, and I'll give mine too
and if it don't work, I'll still, dream about you!!!

[from the 80s]

I will live forever in your dreams
and you, will never replace me
I've been where they're going
and I have seen all they'll see
and I will live for ever in your dreams
you will hold me forever in your arms
I was first to taste the pleasure of your charms
yes, you will hold me forever in your arms
I am a permanent fixture in your mind
I cannot be removed by the test of time
for it was I, that made these feelings start
now, you will hold me forever, in your heart
yes, I will live forever in your mind
but what about me, where am I???

****

"THIS "ole" Show"

this "ole" show has been a long time coming
it got started over 60 years ago
I got sidetracked about 1000 times
made a lot of wrong turns, going to and fro
but they were all important,
especially the ones, that put me in the know
and provided all this verbal deliberation,
substance, for a one-way life of afterglow
all these pieces, written mostly in days of old
each play the part, of a stepping stone
to the achievement, of another goal
which seems a little crazy, or so I'm told
to start a tour at age 80, means I might appear alone
that's okay, cause I'm not counting on tickets sold

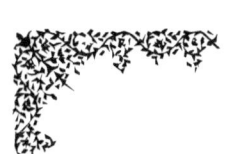

I've already been paid, for the songs
I'll sing and the stories I'll tell
it'll keep my memory from growing cold,
and keep my heart alive and well
so watch for me five years from now, though
I might not be standing with a mic
hell, I might roll in on a motorized hospital
bed, or who knows, maybe on a bike
what ever, you know I will settle for either one
to start a tour at age 80 from a perfect life of fun!!!
It will be called
"This "Ole" Show"
don't miss it – we'll have fun
//because\\
"I WAS BORN FOR FUN"

"Never Again"
5-8-88
[possible song]

now there is something that I miss about you
the part of our love that always leaves me blue
with your love, I knew I'd never win
so I don't think, I'll go back there again
oh so cold – so cold and frigid be
freeze all the love, you held for me
my heart cannot survive another spin
and I don't want to go that way again
I'm left in limbo and afraid
you – will dessert, our love some day
I guess this must be our journey's end
for I never want to go back there again
you have left my heart so hard and sore
I'm not capable of loving like before
now, I don't even want to be your friend
and I don't want to go back there again
oh – no, I never want to go back there again!!!

"I'll Take You, Lonely Or Not"
11-29-1990

oh, I'll take you, lonely or not
if loneliness is all you've got

then I hope, you bring me a lot
yes, I'll take you, lonely or not

I've heard how you treat your lover's heart
please give me a chance to play that part

I have had all the good loves I can take
let me offer you another heart to break

no, I don't have a fortune
but I'll give you all I've got

take my heart, break it, baby give it your best shot
yes I'll take you, lonely or not

now I don't care how much it hurts
drag this "ole" heart through the dirt

for all the mental pain that you inflict
could not compare with my life's tricks

sometimes the thought of mental pain
hastens my decision to remain

just long enough to present, what you haven't got
yes my dear, I'll take you, lonely or not!!!

"Hockey – Tonk State Of Mind"

5-16-2016
[song]

hey, all my mental pain
is soothed by honky-tonk rain

a honky-tonk tornadoe struck
now honky-tonk's – are where I find my luck

'm in a honky-tonk state of mind
maybe someone different could help me find

a way to satisfy
this honky-tonk state of mind

I've been hurting too long now
and there is no one to blame

I'm just trying to burn a candle
that don't even have a flame

so now I'm living in a dream world
and I'll just be taking my time

because the way things are happening
I'm doing just fine – happy all the time

loving and dreaming, in this honky-tonk
state of mind!!!

"A $54 Loan"

[July 1972]

what you say bru
can you loan me two
well you know me
it might take three
I'll probably need more
could you let me have four
maybe spare me five
just to keep me alive
aw – let me have six
so I can get my kicks

just show me that seven
I'll be on my way to heaven
well in case I'm late
ya know it might take eight
will you let me have nine
so I can get a little shine
I said, let may have ten
till I see you again
now that is what be known
as a $54 loan!!!

"Talk To Me Baby"
11-29-73
[song]

ba –by, ba –by, talk to me – baby
may – be – – may – be baby
I'll hear you – – this time

ba –by – – ba –by, talk to me baby
may – be I'll hear you – – this time

I couldn't hear, because my hea – d wasn't clear
and my hea – – rt wouldn't listen
to what it coul – dn't stand to hear

but ba –by, baby baby, may – be maybe
I'll hear you this time

So ba –by, ba –by, plea –se talk to me baby
oh, ta – lk to me baby

and maybe baby, I'll hear you this time
maybe baby – – I'll hear you – this time

what would life be – if not for us
I know without you, my li – fe is – – a bust

So ba –by, ba –by, please ta – –lk to me baby
oh – wont you talk to me baby

and maybe baby, I'll hear you – – this time
may – – be baby, I will hear you – – this time!!!

"My Sweet Little Indian Girl"

{early to mid 60s}
possible song

my sweet little Indian girl
you sure was a pearl

if I could turn the pages back
I wouldn't cut you any slack

but the pages just won't turn
and so my heart does yearn
as memories in my mind, still churn

oh, you sweet little Indian girl
you sure did rock my world

you came to play for just a day
and I'm so glad you passed my way

if I could take another glance
you would never have a chance
you'd be the one I'd take--- to the dance

oh, my sweet little Indian girl
thank you for the mental swirl

with your big brown eyes and cool black hair
you were for sure, my Lady fair

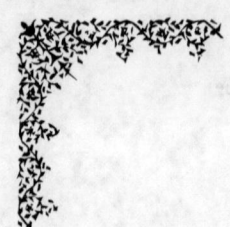

though try-they did, but could not take
you gave to me, what they can't shake
while in dreams of you, I do not wake

with you forever on my mind
our dreams will be there for all time

so I'll drink to us and the things we've done
when taking chances was so much fun

ithout hesitation and not one care
we did what no one else would dare
though now and then we had a scare

which only made, our hearts beat faster
to out of control, where lust was master

we came so close to getting caught
and we're both glad that we did not

now, if I could wrap my life into one world
the wrapping, I know would not come unfurled
you will always be, my sweet, beautiful, little
Indian girl!!!

"Slow Drinking – No Thinking"
11-29-2016
{chorus}

oh, let slow drinking, as I please
help me get up off my – knees
let that girl leave my mind
keep her memory far behind
let the heartstrings – slow re – lease
help the pain in my heart cease
let me have one day of peace
help me hold my heart at ease

*****

it's been a long – long time I know
to keep a love and not let go

not to let old memory's fade
instead, new feelings I have made

if I could on –ly make be –lieve
it's not her lo –ve for which I grieve

maybe then content would come
and my mind would not be numb
{chorus}
oh, let slow drinking, as I please
help me get up off my – knees
let that girl leave my mind
keep her memory far behind
let the heartstrings – slow re – lease
help the pain in my heart cease
let me have one day of peace
help me hold my heart at ease

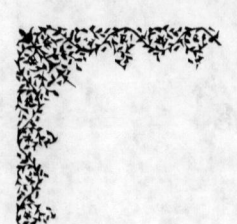

*****

44 – long years and more
all through my life I've kept this torch

it requires refueling of the fire
with memory's of your love desired

it helps me climb up off the cur – –b
out of the gut –ters I preferred

gives strength to stagger up the stairs
believing someone really cares

there I would fall into my bed –
your dreams constant in my head

[repeat in lower tone]
oh – with dreams of you all through my head
{end with chorus}
yes, let slow drinking, as I please
help me get up off my – knees
let that girl leave my mind
keep her memory far behind
let the heartstrings – slow re – lease
help the pain in my heart cease
let me have one day of peace
help me hold my heart at ease
oh, let slow drinking, as I please
help the pain – – in my hea –rt cease!!!

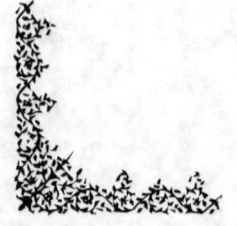

"Take Me Back Mama"

[a mid 60s blues song]
[chorus]

well take me back mama
baby tri-me one more time
we can leave this place together
yeah – – we'll leave it all behind
aw – take me back mama
just one more ti –me
take me back pretty mama
before I lo – –se my mind

*****

I've been thinking about you baby
ever since you went away
yeah – thinkin' since you went away
can't understand you leavin'
so come on back to stay
yeah – take me back mama
baby try me one more time
we can go away together
and leave our troubles behind
ta –ke me back mama
oh – take you back mama
baby try-me one more time
take me back pretty mama
before I lo – –se my mind
now I once had a little gal
lawd she answered to my beckoned call
yeah – once I had a pretty mama
she answered every time I called
I got home late one evening
and saw the writing on the wall

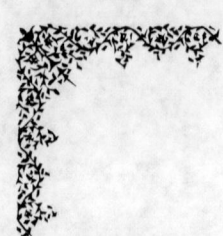

well take me back mama
tell me that you're really mine
we can be together baby
until the end of time
oh – take me back mama
honey – try me one more time
yeah take me back mama
take me back pretty mama
before I lose my mind!!!

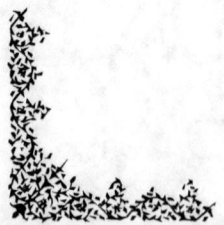

"Lie To Me"

[mid 80s song]
{chorus}

honey, lie to me, lie to me, like you used to do
yeah, make me believe, our love is still true
no don't show me something, I don't want to see
darlin' – don't make me think, that you're leaving me
baby, lie to me, lie to me, sat – is –fy me

*****

you're going shopping with mama
you'll be home before dark
don't tell me your meeting
that man in the park
I hope you buy lots of pretty things
while you're shopping today
for that's what makes you happy
and I like you that way
baby don't make me hear, what I don't want to know
don't make me believe, it's my fault if you go
no, honey don't show me something, I don't want to see

just lie to me, lie to me, honey sat – is –fy me
if I had the power, my life to relive
oh, I do it all over with you
I would not erase, one minute
of the pain that you've put me through
I have loved you so much, for so many years
and I know I can't take, what you want me to hear
so darlin', lie to me, lie to me
don't tell me the truth
don't say anything
to make me think we're through

I know I'll never find anyone
more pleasing than you
so come back home baby
and do what you do
you do it so well, I just don't give a damn
I am lustfully lost, but I am what I am
I'll be listening for a heartbeat
or footsteps so clear
but baby, I don't want to see
what my heart, can't hear
{end with chorus}
so honey, lie to me, lie to me, like you used to do
tell me what you're doing, just isn't the truth
before I close the door, on both of our lives
honey
lie to me, plea –se lie to me, just one more time
"thank you darlin'"
for all the good times!!!

"Get Ready" #1
{baby get ready for me}
3-28-83
written in Montego Bay, Jamaica, for her birthday"
[song]

well let me love you baby, let me love you all night long
I said let me love ya baby, baby – baby all night long
if you let me love you, I'll teach you how to sing my song
it's got that old time rhythm, pullin' on your soul
yeah, got that old blues rhythm baby – pull – pull –
Pullin'at your soul
it fills your heart with freedom
and teaches you to rock 'n roll
yeah – I said let me love you baby
let me love you like I know how –ow –ow
oh let me love you pretty mama
hey – let me love you now –ow –ow –ow
you know I got you honey
gotcha wrapped around my heart – art – art
yeah I really gotcha baby
gotcha wrapped all around my heart
so don't be pulling so hard baby
you're tearing my mind a – part
hey – hey pretty mama, now you let my mind alone
listen to me honey, you better let my mind a – lone
if you don't want what I got for ya
you just carry your sweet – ass home – hell yeah
take all your goodies and go

aw – get ready pretty baby, ready as you can be
you know how to get ready h – o –n –e – y
ready – ready – ready for me
yeah get your self ready mama
honey don't you be late hey – hey
I'm gonna take you to heaven on this very day

rollin' rollin' rollin' baby baby all night long
will get the springs squeakin' honey
eu – e, to the rhythm of our lovin' song
you'll be quiverin' and – a – shakin' and bathing in sweat
I'm gonna give you lovin' you will never forget
so get ready, get ready – ready – ready
baby don't you be late
hey now, I got something for your mama
and you know it just can't wait
oh – you get ready baby
daddy's gonna take you higher
yeah get ready baby –eu – e
you know I'm gonna take you higher
I'm gonna take you so high baby
it'll set your pretty little ass on fire
going to give you good lovin' mama
yeah – baby, gonna take off all your clothes
I'm having you for dinner baby
with straw--berries between your toes
y –e –a –h put you on the dinner table
straw – berries, between your toes
we'll have a lot – a whipped cream
and you know where the cherry goes
so get ready baby, ready as you can be
you better get your self ready
hey, ready – ready – ready for me –eu – e – e
I'm going to take your treasure
replace it with pleasure
you're going to get more lovin' baby
then you can measure
our love will get deeper and better
through the years we'll watch it grow
a – a – w – w baby it gets so much bigger
every time I look at your halo

so get ready – get ready
baby get ready for me
while you're swimming in loves goodies
honey – tell me what you're thinking of
are you capturing the moment
of the deepness of our love
and if you don't think it's deep enough baby
I just give you a little shove
now you're ready baby ready as you can be
aw, yeah I know you're ready – honey
ready – ready – ready for me, alright now
here we go –o–o–o – –eu – e – e – e – e

"Happy Birthday Baby"
*******WHO'S YOUR DADDY*******

"Donna I Don't Wanna"

8-17-88
[song]

hey Donna, I don't wanna – hey Donna, I don't wanna
no, no, no, I don't wanna
don't want to do it again
cause every time we do it
I know damn well I can't win
so Donna, I don't wanna
you know I just don't wanna do it again

I love you baby, love you so much it's a sin
aw but Donna, Donna Donna
I don't wanna, wanna wanna
don't want to do it again

you took my heart, babe you took my soul
you took everything that makes me whole
so Donna, no no no, I don't wanna
don't want to do it again

you took my love, you took my brain
you damn near drove your man insane
and Donna, I don't wanna, do it again

oh, you got the best lovin' I ever had
but when you leave I just feel so bad
so Donna, no no no I don't wanna
don't want to do it again

You tell me you love me with all your heart
then you turn around and tear my world apart
so Donna, I don't wanna, don't want to do it again

no I don't want to do it again
you say that you want to be my wife
and you will love me for the rest of your life
but when that Red Vette cranks, and you drive away
I just can't think of anything to say
except, Donna I don't wanna, no no Donna
I just don't wanna, don't want to do it again
well your body and your booty makes me just
wanna die
and if I try to keep you satisfied
I know I just might
you spread your lovin' feast all night and all day
baby, I just don't understand
how you can walk away
so no no Donna, I don't wanna
don't want to do it again
you haunt me with your body
and your orgasmic charms
it seems like all I live for
is to be in your arms
I have always loved
being under your spell
the price I pay for that
I'll never tell
it could be my mind, my heart or my soul
you know you always make me lose control
but no – more, oh – Donna
you know I don't wanna, don't want to do it again
when you told me goodbye I knew I'd never be free
your memory is always playing round with me

It crawls around on the walls and gets under the cover
and keeps reminding me that you're a special lover
it's been a long long time since you went away
and your memory leaves me only one thing to say

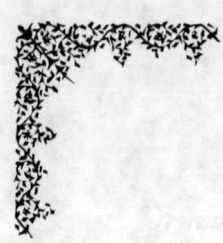

o – –h n – –o Donna
I'm telling you I don't wanna
I don't want to do it again
hey hey Donna, no no I don't wanna
I never want to do it again!!!
"God", I lie like a rug,
anytime you're ready baby

"Gonna Drink Up All The Beer #1"
7-7-78

well this time I'm going to drink up all the beer
they can make in Milwaukee for the next 500 years

I thought this time when you left
I'd know just how to feel

but you left for a different reason
and it started up a brand-new deal

so I'm gonna drink all the beer
in every bar in town

if I drink enough by closing time
maybe I'll get lucky and drown

all the sorrow that you've left me
and the memories of a love so real

yes tonight, old Milwaukee
is gonna change the way I feel

you said this time when you left
you would like to make it clean

now the way you define that word
"ole" Webster's has not seen

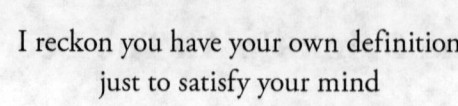

I reckon you have your own definition
just to satisfy your mind

but ever since you've been gone
I've been – a – lookin' for mine

so I think I'll just drink up all the beer
they can make in Milwaukee for the next 500 years

maybe I could find a ho – le, that I could crawl inside
and if it's deep and dark enough, I might be
satisfied
well the last time this happened
they had to start up four new brands

every time you shoot me out – a the saddle
they can't meet my demands

I think I'll move my resident's
to a bar for the rest of the year
cause tonight, I'm gonna drink up all the beer

yes tonight I think I'll drink up all the beer
they can make in Milwaukee for the next 500 years

it will help to ease the pain
and make this heartache disappear
so tonight, I'm – a – gonna drink up all the beer

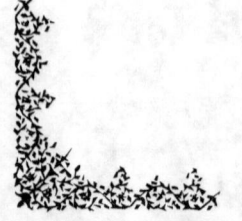
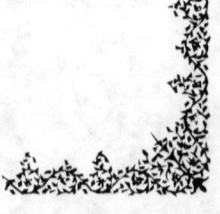

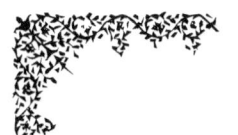

now I just started to believe in you
after what you put me through

then you left me down and out
and – a – frothin' at the mouth
you know it just ain't right my dear

so I called up Milwaukee
so they could get their act in gear

cause this time, you can bet your sweet little ass
I'm gonna drink up all the beer

y –e – a–h, this time I'm gonna drink up all the beer
they can make up in Milwaukee for the next 500 years
it'll help me to forget how you done me wrong
until I read the words in this damn song

but honey I do – not really care
cause tonight I'll be drinking, myself out – a – here
yeah – tonight I'm gonna drink up all the beer!!!
"yes I will – darlin'"

"Get Ready #2"
late 80s

get ready, get ready cause I'm coming
get ready baby cause I'm coming
I'm coming back to you, what goes around comes around
and I'm coming back to you, get ready, get
ready, I'm on my way, get ready, get ready
well you know you're gonna find it's true
if it goes around it'll come around
nd I'm bringing it back to you
get ready, get ready, yeah,
you had me for a while
then you moved on through
but get ready baby, I'm bringing it back to you
get ready, get ready it's, comin', yes it's comin'
it's all coming back to you
well I had you once and I'll get you again
I'll teach you how to separate the boys from the men
get ready, get ready baby
get ready cause it's comin'
yes it's comin'
coming back to you!!!
Get ready baby

"Don't Tell Me Something I Already Know"

6-3-01

[song]

[course]
don't tell me something, I already know
honey, lie if you want to, or say it ain't so
your love has faded, like an old piece of clothes
so don't te – ll me something, I already know

****

I alrea – dy know, that forever's too long
you tau – ght me that, when you left me alone

I know nothings for ever but mom's apple pie
and you'll ne – ver love me till the day that you die

we go throu – gh the motions for all our friends
sake
we've got every – one fooled from the steps that we take
but when all's said and done, and nights curtain falls
I'll be missing the one, that I need most of all
[chorus]
so baby, don't te – ll me something I already know
you can lie if you want to, or say it ain't so
your love has faded, like yesterday's rose
no don't te – ll me something, I already know

****

we had a good love, it should still be going on
and it hurts like the devil, just knowing your gone

we're just biding our time, playing loves game
with a flickering fire, in search of a flame

nighttime brings night dreams, to most lovers hearts
old memory's from our love, push us farther apart

we trusted our happiness, on something once said
and now we are sleeping, in two different beds
[end with chorus]
so baby, don't te ll me something, I already know
you can lie if you want to, or say it ain't so
honey, your love has faded, like yesterday's rose
so don't te – ll me something, I already know
yes your love has faded, like an old piece of clothes
so don't te – ll me something, I already know!!!

"The Boy Wearing Black"

5-16-66
[song]

[chorus]
oh, they call me the bo – y, wearing black
since you're gon – e, and you're no – t coming back
now bla – ck is the color, that forlor – n lover's use
and black, is the color that I choose

****

you went awa – y and left me blue
and all alo – ne, just missing you
without a reason, for what I did, or didn't do
although you kne – w, when you left
that losing yo – u, scared me to death
but I guess it didn't matter
if m – y hea – rt got shattered
all you wan – ted, was to do what you do

And for tha – t I'll give you credit
although I can –'t believe I let it
slip awa – y, like the earl – y morning dew
you took my hea – rt, you took my soul
girl you ma – de, me lose control
and I was los – t in a place, I never knew
wai – ting for a word from yo – u
something ju – st to get me through
or a reason, for m – e to hold on
but that ca – ll, never came
you shut me ou – t, of the game
and left me, just li – ke a lovers pawn

[chorus]
now they call me the bo – y wearing black
since you're gon – e, and you're not coming back
oh – black is the co – lor, that forlorn lover's use
and honey – black, is the color that I choose

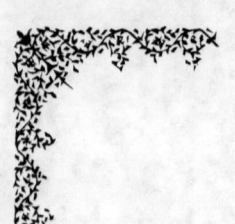

****
I still hold memory's of our love
each night in my dreams
throu – gh the yea – rs
they haven't faded at all
if I get lonesome, for what we had
my memories are never sad
and in my dreams, I can hold you
when you call
oh, I know you – will be with me
throughout all – eternity
you were my first love
and the best one – of all

****

When you slip into, my dreams at night
it's like love at first sight
the way it was, the first day we met
with a passion, we shared together
desires touch, couldn't fee – l any better
when morning comes, I'm covered with sweat
though I no longer hold – you in my arms
I'm still a captive of your charms
I'm just a prisoner, of a love I can't forget!!!

[end with chorus and repeat last two lines]
now they call me the bo – y, wearing black
since you're gon – e, and you're not – coming back
oh bla – ck is the color, that forlor – n lover's use
and black, is the color that I choose
yes bla – ck is the color, that forlor – n lover's use
now black, is the color that I choose

****

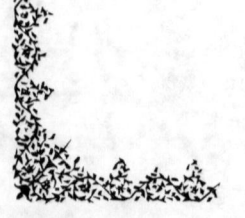

"Red Vette Blues – #2"

3-28-89

well – I got those rock – a – bye baby
you know I love ya maybe
rol – lin' Red Vette blues
you know my baby done left me
la – wd, she left me with nothin' to choose
yeah my baby left me
I ain't go – t no more to lo – se
now I got them rock – a – bye baby
I still love ya maybe
rollin' Red Vette blues
oh yeah – my baby left me
and I ain't got nothing left to lose
she left me with these low down
good for nothing
rollin' Red Vette blues
she just took that little Red Vette
and rolled right outta my life
overnight – yeah – yeah
and when she started rollin'
you know – man – it only took one night
yeah – she was gone a lot faster – than she came by
she left so fast – she didn't – even – see me cry
no no – my baby didn't see me cry
I said – now wait a minute mama
I gotta find – what it is you do
aw baby – you just wait a minute now
I need to know honey – what it is you do
you done put me in a bad – bad – lonesome mood
ya left me moaning
you know you leave your daddy moaning
oh – baby – moanin' these Red Vette blues
da---daa---de–daa–da--de-der

double down and dirty
good for nothin' cotton pickin'
dad – blamed – rock – a – bye baby
rollin' Red Vette blues
baa –baa – be –bop – ba – bop – bop – pow
now if she ever comes back
I know just what I'm gonna do
I'm gonna lock her up real tight
and throw the ke – – y a way too
cause I ain't going through
no – no I don't want to go through
these rock – a – bye baby, rollin' Red Vette blues
no – no no, never again
mercy – have mercy baby – no more
oh – plea – se have mercy baby, for sure
aw – my baby left me – with nothing left to lose
hey – hey, I don't know why
she didn't even say goodbye
now, I got these rock – a – bye baby
you know I love ya maybe
rollin' Red Vette blues
ba – dodi – doe – doe – pa – pa–pa—pa--pop--pop pow
well – – believe me pretty baby
hey hey – listen to me when I say
you gonna be looking for a cookie
and miss your daddy some day
that "ole" cookie jar is empty baby
since you sent your daddy a – way
hey – hey hear what I say
empty – baby, no cookies today
now I woke up this morning
no coffee in my pot
yeah woke up this morning, baby
no coffee in my pot
and I'm looking in the icebox
for something I ain't got hey – hey

oh, I'm living in this room
that just ain't got no door
no way out mama, ain't got no door
ever since you left me honey
my hearts just so damn sore
o – o – h – I miss you baby
you know damn well I do
how come you had to go away
and lea –ve me with these Red Vette blues
I got those rock – a – bye baby
still love ya maybe
rollin' Red Vette blues
oh – boo – hoo – baby – baby
I guess that's just the way life goes
if we are neither here nor there
first your head and then your toes
it really doesn't matter where
and who the hell – really cares
oh – me – oh – my – mama
I had a real good piece of cake
yeah baby, baby, you sure are tasty
a real fine piece of cake
but I ate the whole damn thing
and my sweet tooth – is to blame
oh – my – thinking bout that woman
is going to drive me insane hey – hey
yeah thinkin' bout that woman
is sure gonna drive me insane
now I tried to get that little mama
to do what I wanted her to do
yes I tried to get that little gal
to do all – I wan – ted her to do
but she ran off in that damn Red Vette
and left me these Red Vette blues – boo – hoo
oh – boo – hoo pretty mama, boo – hoo all night long

I've been boo – hoo 'n about you baby
boo – hoo – hoo 'n through this whole damn song
aw – boo – hoo baby, why don't ya come on home
come back to your daddy some – day
come on back pretty – baby
back to your daddy some – day
ya know I'll be lookin' – for you mama
yeah I'll be looking for ya every place
now listen to me baby
I want ya to hear – what your daddy say
aw – listen to me honey, hear what I got to say,
I bought you a brand-new cookie jar, baby
yes I did – and I filled it up – all the way
oh – you left me empty – empty-handed baby
but I'm always dreaming about you
yeah – dreaming about you baby
there just ain't nothing left for me to do
except dream about you baby
while I'm driving around with these
rock – a – bye baby – still lovin' you maybe
"Rolling Red Vette Blues"!!!

"Honky-Tonk Heaven"
4-5-2017
[song]

I want a honky-tonk in heaven
when I cross that great divide

a place to make me feel at home
with the way I've lived my life

there will be no cover charge
no limits, or last call

At the honky-tonk's in heaven
not one tear will ever fall

the honky-tonk's in heaven
will have no closing time

no one to tell you that you
must walk, or toe the line

show me to the dance floor
and put a microphone in my hand

I've got a seat reserved
real close to the band

there's no need to prop me up
you can't drink enough to fall

it all adds up to having fun
it'll be a heavenly ball

there's always been a honky-tonk
no matter where you go

from David and Goliath
to the battle of the Alamo

when victory came, the name of the game
was drink, dance, and celebrate

and like them I feel the same
for this party I can't wait

so if a honky-tonk in heaven
should be my last desire

let the jukebox play until I say
that it sets my soul on fire

yes – I want a honky-tonk in heaven
where all my friends can come

to drink and talk about the fun we've had
and the crazy things we've done

there won't be any crying
or feeling so dog – gone blue

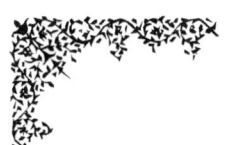
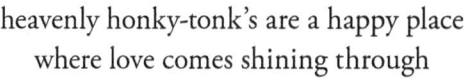

heavenly honky-tonk's are a happy place
where love comes shining through

the bar – tender serves up happiness
and no – body wears a frown

it's the kind of place you can just walk in
and lay all your burdens down
{repeat}
yeah, the bar – tender is serving happiness
and no – body wears a frown

it's the kind of place you can walk into
and lay all your burdens down!!!

"The Blues Must Be Bluer Than Blue"

3-28-88
[song]

[chorus]
oh the blues must be bluer than blue
George sang – about it, and "ole" Hank did to
they both lost – their lovers, like I'm losing you
yes the blues must be bluer than blue

*****

I called up – an old friend, just to ask for some help
he said, listen to me, don't feel sorry for yourself

or you'll end up – in a place, where you don't want
to be
just talking – to yourself, with an old memory

I sent word to – the sheriff, on how things were
being done
he said I'm not – surprised, it could happen to anyone
but don't get – downhearted, true love never fails
in years to come, for what she's done
she'll wear that long black veil
[chorus]
yes the blues must be bluer than blue
George sang – about it, and "ole" Hank did to
they both lost – their lovers, like I'm losing you
yes the blues must be bluer than blue

*****

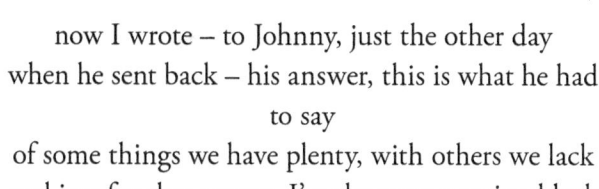

now I wrote – to Johnny, just the other day
when he sent back – his answer, this is what he had
to say
of some things we have plenty, with others we lack
and just for that reason, I'm the man wearing black

If she had not loved you, you wouldn't have what
you've got
you've got a memory of when, she used to love you a lot

not much consolation, if I'm trying to find
the reason I'm feeling, plum out of my mind

so I'll just pull up some memories, and a bottle of Jack
if I can drink long enough, I know she'll be back!!!
[end with chorus]
yes the blues must be bluer than blue
George sang – about it, and "ole" Hank did to
they both lost – their lovers, like I'm losing you
oh yes, the blues must be bluer than blue

*****

"The Mean "Ole" Cleanup Kitchen Blues"

[from the early 80s]

early Sunday morning, dishes everywhere
gotta clean them up so I can put some more there
I don't know where to start, or how long it will take
but these cleanup – up kitchen blues I've got to shake
I've got the mean "ole" clean – up kitchen blues
pom-pom pow pom-pom pow-pa-pa-pow
I gotta shake these blues
yeah – and I gotta shake – em now
oh, listen to me mama, when you see me this way
you're gonna find your daddy missin' someday
these damned "ole" kitchen blues
going to drive your "sugar daddy" away

and I'll be gone, I'll be gone – gone – gone
yeah, your sweet – tooth left you
he just left you hanging on
hanging on to nothing
and now your gonna be alone
stop lying to me baby, I hate the lies you tell
stop lying to me baby, I hate the lies you tell
you know that lying will take you, straight to hell
yeah got hot hot water, hot hot water-suds
these dishes are, covered with crud
hey – hey – – oh – oh
watch the dirty dishes go
and where they go, you never know
they come back so much faster
and every time I ask her
I always get the same answer
it wasn't me, I didn't do it
so, I finally figured out, screw it
{and that's what we did}
it don't matter how I try, or what I do, I just can't

I just can't shake
these damned "ole" clean – up kitchen blues
I got those mean "ole" kitchen clean – up blues
one thing for sure
there is only one cure
hey, rinse me off cutie
I'm coming after your bo-o-ty
I'll cover your rosebud
with a whole bunch-a suds yeah--yeah–yeah!!!

"No Worries"
5-16-85

[chorus]
I can't take time to worry about you baby
I can't take time to think of where you are
no I can't take time to worry about you baby
so I'll just take you, like you are

*****

I'll pretend you're that perfect little angel
that used to run her fingers through my hair

I'll make-believe our love is true and honest
and I am the only one for which you care

with balloons and champagne
laying on a sheepskin rug

waiting for me to open the door
so she could have a hug

or in the middle of the day
wearin' a nighty with white lace

wearin' white just like an angel
and could never be replaced

you always dressed our table like a bed
and dessert, there was plenty of

there was just no way I could go hungry
for you always filled my plate with love!!!
[end with chorus]

"Wastin' Time"
9-10-2016

[a blues song]
you know honey, oh – oh, if you ever change your mi-nd
baby – baby – – oh, I won't, no I won't be
won't be ha – r – d to find

I'll just be sitting here, who – ah– – oh sitting here
a – wastin' time, just wa – stin' time

now may – be you thou – ght I – I – I didn't love you
but you were all – al – l that was ev – er on m – y – mind

so I'm makin' it easy, e – asy, so – so e – – asy for you baby
cause I will be right here, oh – yeah baby – baby,
just wastin' time

o – h you know – I'm going to be right here
yeah – yes you know – your daddy will be right
be right here just wa – stin' time

aw ba – by baby baby, there was no reason,
no – no – no – no reason for leaving
leaving our good lo – ve be – hind

now you don't understand, oh – ba – by please try
try to understand, when it comes to lo – ve
ba – by – baby most men are blind

but let me tell you baby, pre– t – ty baby
ju – st how much you mean, – how much
you mean to my wor – ld
and this otta tell you – eu-u – yeah, make me it plain
to you baby, why I want you,
want you to be my girl

you're the air in my bubble
baby you are the mirror on the wall
you are the dollar sign my bank account
without you my world would fall
you are the clothes that I wear
you are what makes my heart beat
you are the gas in my tank
with – out you – my li – fe is – incom – plete
you are my everything ba – by
from my head, all the way down to my feet
yeah – yeah
but I can't tell you that baby
so I'll write it in this song

one thing you gotta know aw – you need to know honey
a man – never misses what he has – baby baby
until it is all – gone

and that's why I'm here – pretty mama
here in this no – good state – of – mind

and I'm gonna be right here waitin' baby
until you come back to me mama
I'll just be waitin' and wastin' my – time!!!

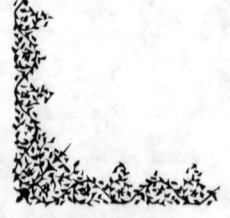
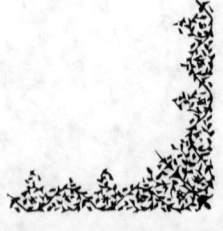

"I've Had Enough Of Your Mental Pain"
[songs from the 70s]

[chorus]
well I've had about enough, of your mental pain
you've created too much, strain on my brain
you make my eyes – fill up with rain
yes I've had about enough, of your mental pain

*****

so why don't you leave, baby leave me alone
go on out and find, yourself another bone

chew up somebody, that likes to be bit
you're just a bad habit, that I'm trying to quit

too many times, you brought love my way
you know it don't seem right, that you're gone to stay

but some way I'll thank "God", for today
and the rest of my life, I know I'll have to pay

yes I'll pay for the love, that I didn't need
pay for a love, that sowed a bad seed

yeah I'll pay for a love, that tore me all apart
and pay for the love, that broke my heart
[chorus]
oh I've had about enough, of your mental pain
you've created too much, strain on my brain
you make my eyes, fill up with rain
and I've had about enough, of your mental pain

well I told you this time, when you slammed the door
that I don't want to see you, back here no more

now it ain't no lie, child I'd rather be dead
it feels like something's blowing, off the top of my head
baby you got good loving, it couldn't get any better
but you know your love, keeps me under the weather
oh it made me feel good, laud, it made me feel bad
you gave me the best, and the worst I ever had

oh well I want no more, to ever fall in love
baby when you come to me, it's like putting on a glove
to go on from here, I'd have to settle for less
but I am gonna stop right here, and ended up with the best
[chorus]
but I'm so damn tired, of your mental pain
you have created too much, strain on my brain
Lord –, you made my eyes, fill up with rain
so give me more, more, more, of your mental pain
"aw baby baby baby, give me more of that pain"!!!

"Sing Your Daddy's Song"

[from the 70s]

Sing your daddy's song – son
sing each line with a smile

you know he lived it all – boy
and he made it all worthwhile

although you may wonder
and sometimes make a blunder

just sing it loud
and sing it proud
your living out his plan

don't think about where you're going
cause you have no way of knowing
you're an extension, of your daddy's hand

You sang your daddy's song – Ted
you sang your daddy's song

you didn't cry when life slipped out of place
you put it back where it belonged

you solved all life's problems
right straight from the heart
with the mind control to never
let another problem start

yes, you sang your daddy's song – Ted
you sang your daddy's song!!!

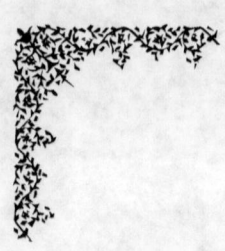

"Slipping way"

slipping away, slipping away
honey I feel our love, is slipping away

things aren't the same, as we used to know
seeds of distrust, are starting to grow

loose tongue destruction is common as day
it results in a love to start slipping away

we should pay no attention
to what the gossip lines read

their lives aren't worth living
if they can't sow bad seeds

just know that I love you
and look for a better day

baby let's stop our love
from slipping away

when we first fell in love
it was a for – ever thing

and we couldn't wait
for the happiness it would bring

some people we knew
didn't want it that way

and they caused our love
to start slipping away
*** finish this***

"Take It Round The World"

[from the 80s]
song

[chorus]
yeah, gonna take it round the world one more time
show a whole lot of women I'm the lovin' kind
have a bunch – a fun spending my last dime
while I'm trying to regain my crown
yes I'll take it round the world just one more time
and then I'll lay my body down

*****

I'm gonna take it round the world one more time
and then I'll lay my body down
I'm getting sick and tired of just hangin'
and waiting for the comings of around
when you administer your justice
I am the recipient of pain
I feel like I fell off – a loves highway
and I'm standing in the pouring rain
I've been – ' waitin' too long now
for the memory's of your lovin' sounds
I'm gonna take it round the world just one more time
and then I'll lay my body down
[chorus]
yeah, gonna take it round the world one more time
show a whole lot of women I'm the lovin' kind
and have a bunch of fun spending my last dime
while I'm trying to regain my crown
yeah I'll take it round the world just one more time
and then I'll lay my body down!!!

*****

www.ingramcontent.com/pod-product-compliance
Lightning Source LLC
Chambersburg PA
CBHW052056070526
44584CB00017B/2213